MW01710422

Miracles Because Jesus Cares

Helen M. Petipren

Miracles Because Jesus Cares

Helen M. Petipren

Copyright © 2004
All Rights Reserved

PUBLISHED BY:
BRENTWOOD CHRISTIAN PRESS
4000 BEALLWOOD AVENUE
COLUMBUS, GEORGIA 31904

Dedication

I affectionately dedicate this book to all of my children, Susan, Barry, David, Debbie, and Tom, and in loving memory of my sister, Bethy.

Acknowledgements

This book has been a labor of love led by the Holy Spirit, to glorify the Miracle Worker, Jesus Christ. It also shows how much He cares for us.

My thanks are given to each one who contributed in helping me make this book become a reality.

I thank David C. Petipren, my son, who continually encouraged me to write it.

Reverend Betty Pelon was invaluable in helping me coordinate and organize the material in preparation for publication. I am thankful for her prayers and encouragement.

My hope is that the book will inspire you, build you up to receive miracles in every area of your life. Jesus is a miracle working God. Miracles are for today. Nothing is impossible or too hard for God. He cares, truly cares for you.

Table of Contents

Preface

One night the Holy Spirit spoke to me Psalm 96:3 LB, "Publish His glorious acts throughout the Earth. Tell everyone about the amazing things He has done." For over 30 years Jesus has performed continuous miracles in my life, family and with others. He has constantly shown me His great love and He has proved to me how much He cares about our every need. (I Peter 5:7) "Let Him have all your worries and cares for He is always thinking about you and watching everything that concerns you." In the King James Version it says "He cares for you."

Jesus is our healer, deliverer, Savior, Miracle Worker, and provider. These chapters show a variety of marvelous miracles the Lord performed. In Psalm 77:14 it states, "You are a God of Miracles." Miracles described include healing of my heart from heart congestion, death bed miracles, recovery and life restoration of my six year-old son from a terrible night of drowning, multiplying of oat field for a financial miracle, and free gas for our 2600 square foot house for over 20 years. Other miracles described are a talent of music miracle, healings of eyesight (dyslexia) and back paralysis of my son, salvation miracles, impossible adoption of a baby from Calcutta, India, creative miracles in Israel, ICU baby resuscitated four times from death and totally healed, how I became a scholar after being disabled and having had eight surgeries. Even thumbs were healed in six days after being cut off by an electric saw. These were impossible circumstances. Doctors could not help. Only God could do the impossible. In Matthew 19:26 "With men this is impossible but with God all things are possible." God's power is greater than any problem we have.

This book will build up those in desperate needs and show that miracles are for today in every area of life. These tremendous testimonies will relate to non-believers and believers of all ages and show that Jesus cares. It proves that God keeps His promises in His Word. The miracles are evidence of God's everlasting love for those who have faith in Him and His Word.

My goal in this book is to offer hope to the helpless, to people with impossible circumstances, to inspire others to have faith in God and never to give up! It is intended to glorify Jesus and show God's great love and that Jesus truly cares about us. The word in Psalm 136:4 LB states, "Praise Him alone. He does mighty miracles, His loving kindness continues forever."

Introduction

Psalm 96:3-4 LB "Publish His glorious acts throughout the Earth. Tell everyone about the amazing things He does. For the Lord is great beyond description, and greatly to be praised. Worship only Him among the gods!"

The Lord Jesus has given me 20 years of miracles. By the grace, goodness, and love of God, He has never failed to meet my needs and more! (II Cor 9:8) He has healed me from so many diseases, delivered me from the hand of the enemy. He has continually blessed my family and friends with miracles. I truly embrace God's miracles as a Christian because I know that Jesus cares about me. (I Peter 5:7)

I have learned to have faith in God, obey His Word, believe His promises are for me, and to worship the Lord of Lords. It is with a thankful heart that I dedicate this book of testimonies to the glory of Jesus Christ.

Oral Roberts taught me to expect (believe) in miracles and that nothing is impossible with God. Dr. Mike Murdock taught me how to sing praises to the Lord through every trial and tribulation until the victory was won. Brother C.H. Weldon encouraged me to answer the call of ministry when it was not popular for women to be in ministry. Pastors Bobbie and Earl Moore mentored me in ministry to equip and build up the body of Christ.

Over 10 years ago, the Holy Spirit instructed me to publish some of these wonderful testimonies. Some are miracles of healings, special gifts and talents, lives saved spiritually and physically, financial victories. Every miracle has been a great gift from God.

Do you need a miracle today? Never give up! Miracles are here for you today. God want you to know what he has done for me He will also do for you, no matter how big or small the need, God loves you and it gives Him pleasure to bless you. Confess and empty all your heart of any doubt, fear, and worry. Give it to Jesus now. Have faith in God. God is so very good and He cares. Yes, Jesus cares about you and all that concerns you.

Through the anointing of the Holy Spirit, you will find encouragement, hope in Christ, faith in God to see real miracles in your own life and circumstances. May every word of this book bring glory and honor to Jesus Christ, my Lord.

The Well of Blessings

Phil. 4:19 "But my God shall supply all your need according to his riches in glory by Christ Jesus."

After living in a small town for three years and surviving continuous gossip and observation by the town's people, we decided that it was time for some privacy. One of our curious neighbors could be found chasing her cat up our tree or in the loft of our garage with a ladder, the person even made it up to the top of our roof. After three years of calling the police, fire department, and Detroit Edison to remove this person from the garage, trees, roof, we wanted a rest from neighbors! The other neighbor thought that she was invited to dinner everyday and she thought she was suppose to plan the menus by checking out my cupboards, refrigerator, taking our phone calls, checking our mail, all without our consent. I wanted to be a good country neighbor but this meant no privacy. One night, we were awakened by party goers lying on our front lawn. At first, we thought this was a nice, quiet, friendly town and most of the people were very nice to us. Maybe these incidents were too friendly for us. So we decided to go out and get some land and build our dream house. The first thing I did was to plant hundreds of seedlings (trees) just in front of the existing trees, near the rear of the property. Next we built a pole barn. Then we literally began breaking ground ourselves with our backhoe for footings for the house. We proceeded very well with construction. My Father-in-law and relatives who needed work assisted. We even had a group of Christian singers who were brick layers. (This was their trade). Soon we were starting inside construction. One day while I was cleaning up some building materials, a plain blue car pulled up to the house. The person driving was alone. He came up to the house and asked whom I was? Then he presented me with some papers and informed me that our house and land were condemned in the public interest. He stated that I must sign the papers he had or lose the house. He also stated that we did not have any property rights. Then he went out to his car and brought in his typewriter. He said all the property rights of the entire area were sold. I told him that that was impossible because I had delayed the closing of the sale of the property for an hour while our attorney checked out the property rights with the recorder of deeds. No sale of storage or mineral rights had been recorded. We were informed that we had title to them. The Holy Spirit quickened to me again to check out the papers and title search. Everyone became quite upset with me for delaying the proceedings. Also, I noticed the sellers were nervously pacing and smoking one cigarette after another. I did not know why they acted this way at the time. According to all the records we had the mineral and storage rights. Well back to the unidentified man who was pressuring me to sign his paper. I told him outright to "leave" and that I would check this out with my husband and an attorney. Next, I called my husband. Boy, he was upset. After talking with the attorney we decided to go to court. We waited anxiously for the court to respond. My husband became so disturbed by the situation that he could not continue with the house. So he stopped all work on the house.

Within a couple of weeks, we received a court summons, but in the meantime, this unidentified man continued to harass me by phone and home visits to try to get me to sign his papers. He became very loud and threatening. Approximately 100 other property owners had also received court summons, notifying them that their property was condemned. I decided to find out the extent of this situation. I made calls to everyone on the list. I was shocked to learn that 12,000 acres had been bought up out here for storage wells. Through further investigation, I found that this company had paid approximately one dollar per acre for the property rights through intimidation, harassment, and fear tactics.

Prior to the invasion to steal property rights, natural gas was extracted and the wells were producing at 90%. These 12,000 acres were a massive natural gas reservoir.

I called every prayer group around the country and seriously sought the Lord for direction. The next day I believe the Lord led me to call a property owner's town meeting. I notified state representatives and senators. I had an old ditto machine and notified everyone in the area about the meeting. About 200 people showed up. The company sent executives and lawyers.

We found favor with the state representative to help us in this battle. He received many phone threats for assisting us. We wrote letters to the editors of several newspapers who printed the letters. Then we were blessed to find a gas well attorney.

One-hundred property owners decided to be supportive of our case action. Twenty-seven of them filed affidavits to the Attorney General's office that confirmed how the property rights were obtained using harassment and intimidation. The Holy Spirit assured us that we would not lose our property and would have victory.

Before we went to court, the company sent out executives to my house, driving big black cars. They tried to get me to sign the papers. I recorded their meetings with me. I soon learned that our property was a main link for the pipeline company and it was necessary to continue their work.

Then the Holy Spirit led me to call a TV station and inform them of what was happening up north. I had to be bold as a lion, since the local news media made a joke of the entire situation. Within an hour and a half, the TV crew came out to my husband's office where I worked. We proceeded to the house where the cameramen shot footage inside and outside and also of documents. They interviewed me about the situation. Our story was put on the telecast with full coverage just proceeding the exclusive news of Elvis Presley's death. Therefore, they had a greater viewing audience than a normal telecast.

In court, the company had ten attorneys, but we had one and the Lord, our defender. The Lord told me not to fear them that He was our attorney. It felt like a Goliath episode. The Judge had already decided in favor of the company before the hearings of the property owners. How could God turn this mess into a miracle?

Well, I felt led to find the headquarters of this big company. So, I took my two children downtown where their office was listed. I found out that it was a dummy office. I stopped and asked the Holy Spirit what to do? He reminded me that I knew a Christian who worked for this company. I went to the elevator captain and asked him to help me find my friend because we were going to surprise him. God gave me favor! The elevator captain called up to my friend's office and guess what?? We were invited to the secret offices. My friend asked how I found him? I said the Lord did it! This friend turned out to be a secret agent for the Lord for us. He had geological reports that stated the wells were in operation at 90% or better, but one of the corporations of this company had shut the wells down for 58 days. Then the company had their geologist state that these wells were operating at less than 25% efficiency so they could be condemned in the public interest. This gave us facts of the deceit of this company. The newspapers ate up the information. The Judge still ruled in the company's favor. The Judge had made his decision even before the hearings.

I went back to the Lord and asked Him what to do next. He told me we would have the victory. It looked impossible. I believe in the God of miracles, the God of impossibilities.

The Lord led me to contact the Attorney General's office again. The example the Lord gave me for consumer protection was this: Magazine salesmen cannot come to your home and harass you so don't allow this deceitful, greedy company to. The Attorney General's office investigated and determined that "the rights were fraudulently obtained by the company." The company was fined and a precedent was set against the company.... the first one on record!

The Attorney General's office said the company had to make restitution to the property owners, but only those that filed affidavits with us. The Lord told me to accept free gas for the rest of my life for my house. Gas was cheap then. That next year prices of natural gas skyrocketed and continued to rise for years after. My house is approximately 2600 square feet. Thanks be to God I have never had to pay a gas bill since. Not only were we also financially compensated, but the company had to pay all attorney fees of $5000. So God kept His word. He blessed a lot of people and gave us the victory. We serve a great and mighty God!

Thumbs Up For Jesus

Luke 1:37 KJ "For with God nothing shall be impossible."

Isaiah 53:5 KJ "But he was wounded for our transgressions, he was bruised for our iniquities ~ the chastisement of our peace was upon him ~ and with his stripes we are healed."

My mother-in-law was helping my father-in-law with some remodeling in the basement. She was holding a piece of paneling which my father-in-law was sawing. Suddenly, the safety failed and while she was holding the wood, the saw backed up cutting off both of her thumbs. I received the call that afternoon of the accident and was asked by my sister-in-law to pray and come down to the hospital.

When I arrived, the hospital staff would not let me see her. I knew the Holy Spirit wanted me to pray directly with her. By God's grace we got a staff member to let me in a side door. Mom was lying on a stretcher, and dad was standing beside her. He could barely speak because he was so upset. I immediately felt the presence of God. As I prayed with her, she felt a sensation of heat cover her body as I laid hands on her and prayed. The pain left her. The nurse checked her blood pressure and it had come down to a safe range. It had been going over 300 before prayer and a stroke or heart attack was feared, but now it was ok. Jesus had touched her and healed her. The Lord said before the week ended she would be able to use her thumbs. Oh, how wonderful God is.

That night I shared the message of salvation with my father-in-law. He prayed for forgiveness and accepted Jesus as his Savior. I encouraged him in the Word of the Lord and prayed for him to forgive himself for the accident. This was a great miracle, and I rejoiced in the Lord. The devil meant it for a tragedy and the Lord turned it all into victories. God is so good to us. How can I express what joy it is to have a family member you love receive the salvation of the Lord. It's so special. God really cares about our loved ones. Keep praying for their salvations, and never give up hope. God will make a way and answer your prayer.

The sixth day after the accident Jesus manifested the miracle. My mother-in-law was able to wash dishes and had no pain. She continued to increase the use of the thumbs. The doctors were truly amazed. The doctors said this was impossible, but we know with God all things are possible. Hallelujah! This occurred over 15 years ago. She received a miraculous healing and the doctors agreed! She was able to return to doing handwork, sewing, needlepoint, and all her favorite hobbies. She would raise her thumbs up everywhere when she told them what Jesus did for her. Praise God!

Now God was not through with the miracles. Mom told her brother about her miracle. He had made fun of our faith for years, but this time he was ready to listen. Doctors had found cancerous tumors on his neck and body. He called me to come pray for him.

His wife and daughter were with him when I arrived to pray with him. I shared the salvation message and all three people accepted Jesus as their Savior and Lord. Mom's brother confessed that he had heard the salvation message before but never received it. This time he really knew it was for him.

Next, I prayed for his healing in Jesus' name. His tumors began to shrink before my eyes. Surely, the Lord Jesus had touched him. He described a warm feeling going through his body. He went to five doctors afterwards, but the tumors were gone. Jesus is the healer. This all occurred while I was divorced from my husband. This was his family God ministered to. God is so kind and merciful. He gave me so much love for them and allowed me to bring them Jesus.

Healing of Heart

Psalm 57:7 KJ "My heart is fixed O God, my heart is fixed, I will sing and give praises."

In 1986, I had been through a series of surgeries from the accidents of 1984 and 1985. A couple of months after ankle surgery, I developed a rapid heartbeat, chest pains, difficulty in breathing and an abnormal EKG. I was sent to University Hospital in Ann Arbor for tests and treatment.

I recall the desperate battle of fear I faced as I lay alone all day and night in the hospital bed with tubes everywhere. It was a private room, with gray walls, and a very lonely room. I could hear the cries and screams of other patients. I listened to the doctors tell me that my tests were not good and I was not in good health.

My husband drove me to the hospital, but remained a very short time. I asked him if he had prayed for me, but he had not. He seemed unconcerned about my condition just like a cab driver would. There wasn't any prayer partner, family, or friend to comfort me, but I knew Jesus was present. I wondered if this was it. Why did God let this happen to me? Tom was only about 7 years old. It was such a torturous night. I just kept calling on Jesus. EKG's continued to be bad. Surely, the Lord would deliver me from this nightmare.

I was scheduled for a heart catherization and balloon treatment that morning. They kept delaying my procedure. This only added to my fear. I somehow managed to untangle my wires for the heart monitor and IV and get the phone. I called Oral Roberts Prayer Tower. The partner bound the spirit of fear and prayed with me. I opened my Bible and it was Psalm 57:7. The Lord FIXED my heart, and I knew the Holy Spirit had given me this word and I would be okay. I felt such thankfulness to the Lord for speaking healing to me.

Right after this, a nurse came in and hooked potassium to my IV. It was so strong that it burned my arm along the vein. I was in tears with the pain but no one would listen to me. I even tried to take the IV out myself. The nurse told me I was just over anxious about the procedure. By the time I got to the surgical room I was passing out and felt very strange. I heard the doctor yelling at the staff about who put me on the wide-open potassium IV. He swore at the staff and the IV potassium was stopped stat! I was given some adrenalin and other medications.

I kept trying to tell them I was healed. They did all the tests and could not find the blockages they were convinced existed. Jesus fixed my heart was all I could say. It seems strange now but during my recovery from the procedure a very young nurse came in my room and prayed with me and had words of comfort. I never saw her before this and never saw her again. I just knew I needed someone and God sent her to me. I felt such peace with her as if she were an angel.

My most precious daughter took off from college and arranged for a driver to come to the hospital to be with me. Susan is the daughter every mother wishes for. She is loving, beautiful, talented, an achiever, brilliant French Hornest, conscientious, leader, always there to help me. She is advocate of justice and truth, basically one of the hardest working, diligent young woman of her day and I could go on.

The next day, the doctors told me that they found my heart to be free of blockage and working very well, but to be sure they wanted another test done which consisted of passing wires through my heart. This did not sound to good to me, but they assured me it was very safe and this way I would be thoroughly checked out. So I agreed to show them that I was healed.

I was taken by wheelchair to the procedure. I even got up on the table myself. The procedure was long, the room was cold, and

I could not move. I was alone, no nurse in attendance through most of it. I could feel my heart going different speeds. The heaviness became unbearable, I called to the doctor to stop, but no one replied. Suddenly, I felt strange and I could not breathe. I could not feel my body. I could see me lying there. I asked the Lord what happened. I remember the doctors yelling she must have had a stroke. I was not afraid. It was strange to just be looking down at myself. I could see myself moving away from my body. I asked the Lord if it was my time. They shot all kinds of medication into me to get me back breathing, and the EKG stabilized. I told the Lord I could not die or leave now, but I just felt His peace. I remember calling out to Jesus to let me live.

Finally, I could feel my body, but I could not yet move. The next day, I heard the top doctors yelling at the staff doctors and swearing as to whether they were trying to keep me alive or dead.

I knew the devil had used these times to try and kill me, but I also knew the Lord Jesus fixed my heart and gave me life. I left the hospital with my heart fixed, not by a gifted doctor, but by the Lord, the greatest physician in the Earth and heaven. They could not explain what happened to me but God can... He gave me a miracle healing!!!!!

A Miracle For Nina

Matthew 19:14 KJ "Jesus said, 'Let the little children come to me and don't prevent them. For of such is the kingdom of heaven'"

A Christian couple decided to adopt a foreign child since they were not able to adopt an American child for a number of years. There was so much red tape and expense with the American adoption. God opened a door for them to adopt an abandoned baby out of Calcutta, India. It is legal for mothers to legally abandon their children there, if they sign a document to intent. My friends learned that there was a baby girl that was abandoned and could be adopted. Through an Evangelist Missionary from Phoenix, they were able to make contact with an attorney in India.

During August, Sister Sue received a letter that certain adoption papers required the Consulate General of India's seal in order to adopt this 8 month-old baby girl who was still in Calcutta.

We were informed that we had one day to do this or lose the adoption. We were informed to bring the papers to Chicago the next day so that they could be postmarked that same day to make this adoption official. So, we prayed and then called the Consulate office in Chicago. The Consulate said, "You must come tomorrow." The Holy Spirit gave us a word to go and He said all these things would be accomplished for His glory that very day.

So, we drove all night from Michigan to Chicago. When we arrived in Chicago at the Consulate General's office, it was locked, closed!!! The offices were dark. No one was there. We repeated the word the Lord had spoken to us and claimed victory. We prayed, "In the name of Jesus, these doors shall be opened and this work completed."

Immediately within seconds of saying the prayer of faith, a foreign looking man stepped out of the elevator. Praise Jesus, he had come to the Consulate office to get some papers. He was the official. We followed him into the office and explained the situation and need. (We prayed for the man to have a compassionate heart and to help us). He apologized for the office being closed, but explained this was the Indian Independence Holiday (like our fourth of July). He also told us that two signatures were required for this adoption document. He said the other Consulate was celebrating the holiday, but he would try to find him. So he made many calls for two hours. We were busy praying in the Spirit in another room as we waited hopefully.

Another couple of hours passed by. Praise God the other Consulate with the seal of authority arrived at the office. Both men were very happy to assist us in this cause. They approved the papers, and put on the necessary seals and signatures.

Now we had 15 minutes to get the papers postmarked that day. Five minutes before the post office closed for the weekend, we got the papers postmarked and mailed.

"Only Jesus the Miracle Worker can make the impossible happen" (Matthew 17:20). We had favor with these Indian Consulates to accomplish God's work. (Ps 5:12, Proverbs 3:4) This occurred in August, and Nina was due to arrive in September. The people of Calcutta rejoiced saying this was a miracle because it takes weeks and months usually to get any paperwork approved by the Consulates. This was the beginning of the vision for a foreign adoption agency in Phoenix and Michigan. Another miracle thanks to Jesus our Lord.

Miracle Harvest of Oats

Deuteronomy 7:13 KJ "I and He will love you, bless you and multiply you. He will also bless the fruit of your womb and the fruit of your land, your grain and your new win and oil, the increase of your cattle and the young of your flock, in the land which He swore to your fathers to give you."

It was the early fall and I had a new baby boy just out of the hospital intensive care unit. It was then that my husband left me for an exotic dancer, and my 17 year-old Sister had recently been murdered in Detroit. My other two children were very distressed about the circumstances. They were having problems and there was no family to comfort them. My friends withdrew from us because they did not know how to react. So, I drew very close to the Lord. I could not understand how so much could go wrong! I had been faithful to the Lord. I had asked for forgiveness (if I had sinned) and repented of any and everything I could think of.

I had been holding prayer meetings at my home, as in the Book of Acts. I had prayer intercessors interceding for my situation. Surely, God had a plan. I refused to put all my energy in depression and self-pity. I wanted my life to glorify the Lord and to give testimony of His mercy, love and miracles. The Lord gave me strength in my weakness. I truly did not know if I could endure all of this, but I knew Jesus cared about me so I could not give up.

The Holy Spirit had spoken to my heart about holding public worship meetings. I certainly did not have the funds or know anyone who would help. At this time, I was taking care of a home of forty acres and an old farm. We rented the farm and the renters planted oats. We were to get half the proceeds from the oat crop.

The renters greatly damaged the farm so they were forced to leave. So I called a crop sharer to look at the oat crop. As a Christian brother, he was truthful and said the crop was "poor to none" and he did not want to take my money or waste his time, but he would take what he could salvage. Other farmers looked at the oat crop and they said the same. I knew that I had to trust the Lord and the harvest. I promised the Lord that if He would bless the crop, I would organize the praise meetings and plant the money from the harvest of oats back into His work.

Two weeks later, the sharecropper called me and asked me to come to the bank. All I thought was how could I pay him now? When I arrived, he handed me hundreds of dollars and he had already taken his share! He said that he had been a farmer for years and he could not believe his eyes. The oats just kept multiplying "just like a miracle!"

At this time in this little country town of twelve hundred people there were four bars, one advertised topless dancers, and a prostitute hotel. One bar owner had a total of seven husbands and six of them had disappeared. There had been several suicides, in fact a man hung himself just a few doors away. There were unexplainable accidental deaths of a number of children. Even though there were a handful of houses on my block, one was dealing drugs. This town had the highest rate of alcoholism in the country and a high divorce rate. Many farmers were losing their land, and there was an arsonist who destroyed a number of businesses. The entire business district was only a block and a half long. Even the minister's house was burned out!

I prayed we could bring the people to Jesus, especially the young ones. Only a few of the children knew about Jesus or anything about the Bible. I prayed for God's mercy and forgiveness for this area.

Praise God, I set up a meeting at the town hall. We put up signs all over town "Praise meeting for Jesus". The meeting was announced on television for two weeks. A busload of people came from Detroit to join us in prayer. A Detroit Christian television network sent Evangelists. A church pianist volunteered to play piano and my children and friends set up chairs and equipment. We even had refreshments. We had over a hundred people attend the first meeting and that's a crowd in the country. This meeting was a victory for Jesus. Many were saved and set free. Finally, the light of His Word had come to this dark area. Praise God there was enough money for more meetings and I set up several meetings at town hall. At last, the prayer warriors came to possess the land for the Lord and break the strongholds of the enemy.

The Holy Spirit gave me comfort and strength to go on in my trials. I felt such unspeakable joy and peace, and all of this came from a harvest of oats blessed by God's miracle power.

The Miracle of Tom

Matthew 10:8 "Heal the sick, cleanse the lepers, raise the dead, cast out devils: freely ye have received, freely give."

As prophesied, I had become pregnant in spite of tumors and other female problems. I was sent to a psychiatrist when I insisted I was pregnant. Doctors had told me to have a hysterectomy and I scheduled the surgery, but when the Lord spoke to me and told me I would conceive a boy child and be healed I cancelled the surgery.

I was already three months pregnant. I did not believe in abortion. I chose to honor the Lord and have this baby, a gift of God. I had to have a Cesarean Section. The Lord gave me the name Thomas John and said that he would be a double blessing of God and serve the Lord and bring me joy all the days of my life.

Thomas John was over 8 lbs when he was born by C-section. He looked great, but suddenly after one hour, the doctors rushed him to intensive care with respiratory distress. He was kept alive on life support. They did not know what happened. Four times the doctors resuscitated him back to life. His little head was full of IV's, and there were tubes everywhere. After many days I was allowed to visit him.

We asked everyone to pray for a miracle. I kept telling the doctors he would live by faith in God. I laid hands on him and prayed for his healing. A few moments after my prayer, Thomas was breathing by himself. I knew he was healed. The doctors observed him and removed him from the respirator. Praise God!!

Also, when I was in the hospital, my husband had a psychiatrist speak to me. The doctor was a Christian and a PTL partner.

He said all I needed was a rest from my husband and his adulterous lifestyle. I cried because I could not understand why this was happening.

I had Christians pray with me at the hospital and called churches and asked for prayer. We had no insurance and the hospital bill was $16,000, but we knew God had blessed us with His miracle.

Thomas had lost over two pounds in intensive care. He did not have a sucking reflex because he received feedings through a gavages tube since birth. The doctors wanted to observe him for thirty days. They were surprised by this miracle healing.

I visited Thomas John (Tom) every couple of days even though I had complications from the C-section. I was finally able to bring Tom home, but only for a couple of days. I was a pediatric nurse in the past, so they showed me how to do gavages feedings. I carefully recorded vital signs, feedings, and medical care. I fed him every two hours and prayed that God would heal him again. Everyday a public health nurse stopped by to check on us.

Five days later, I took Tom back to the hospital. When they weighed him, he was above birth weight. His lungs were clear and he was strong and healthy. The doctors said this was impossible, and I said it was a miracle!! The doctor agreed and wrote on Tom's chart "God's Miracle". I took Tom home.

The head of the neonatal clinic was a doctor I had dated when I was in my nursing training. This doctor's father was Muslim Bishop in Iraq. Tom's healing was a testimony to him because he could not deny that my God had given me a miracle.

Tom never suffered any problems from his early illness. He was an all A student and continues to receive high honors. He scores high in math and graduated June 1997. He even took some college course when he was a high school senior. He is a gifted musician and plays guitar and trumpet. He is just what the Lord said, "A joy in my life."

Miracles in Israel

James 1:22 KJ "Obey the message, be doers of the word, not merely listeners, betraying yourself"

John 14:23 IB "Because I will only reveal myself to those who love me and obey me. The Father will also love them too and we will come to live with them."

Mark 11:22-24 KJ "And Jesus replying said to them, have faith in God constantly! Truly I tell you, whosoever says to the mountain, be lifted up and thrown to the sea! And does not doubt at all in his heart, but believes that what he says will take place, it will be done for him.

I was praying to the Lord and heard a word from the Holy Spirit, God "hear the word of the Lord and obey it." I was not sure what this meant at first. I used to sing a little song that I would go anywhere God wanted me to, cross the great oceans, climb the high mountains. Well God must of heard me because on May 18, 1980, I arrived on Televive. This was my first airplane ride anywhere. We arrived first in Boston after cruising at 37,000 feet. We were on the Swissair plane for hours traveling 540 miles and hour at 3000 feet and we were crossing the Atlantic Ocean. I sang a lot of praises to the Lord through the flight. This was a ride of faith for me. At one point, I wondered how I ever decided to go to Israel. I really knew very little of its history other than Jesus lived there and the Old Testament heroes lived there.

One day the Holy Spirit spoke to my heart about a trip to Israel. My lady friend was going. I thought, no way. I have a year old baby, just divorced, two other children and no money for our needs. So, I hesitantly asked the Lord to provide the funds and a sitter that I could trust with my children. Soon after that, a man knocked on my door and asked to buy my trees. I use to own 40 acres of land with woods. His offer was good, but the Lord said to wait. My sisters and brothers in the Lord encouraged me that God really wanted me to be one of the eleven on this special trip. Next thing I knew, a Christian man asked to buy my trees and offered double what the first man offered. Then to my surprise, my mother volunteered to take care of the children so I could go to the Holy Land.

For me to go was an act of obedience to the Lord. I tried not to think of all the reason why I should not do this. Of course, it did not make sense in the natural, but here I was with my one suitcase on a deluxe aircraft going to the Holy Land. I did not even know most of the people that I was going with except they were Christians. All I knew was that I had better of heard the Holy Spirit. The prophecy for the trip was that only eleven would go and the leader of the trip, as a special delegation for the Lord. I surely had mixed emotions, but I knew in my heart the Lord had spoken and I wanted to obey even if I did not understand and really did not want to fly. I figured that I can fly when Jesus comes.

A gentleman in our group sat next to me. He was as scared as me about flying, so we decided to sing praises as long as we could. Everyone else knew this was our first flight and so they began to sing with us. We both said that the flight was great as soon as we landed safely. The leader to the group laughed. He was a pilot and said it was pretty rough.

Well, it was May 19, 1980 when we arrived in Israel. We had been searched, and searched and even strip-searched. We were taken to a hangar. Our luggage was taken from us. Soldiers with guns stood around us. This looked like serious business here. No one had warned me about this. We were led to a plane hangar and told nothing. Then at the next point, we were given a strip search. I began to have some anxiety about this trip already and I had not seen anything outside the hangar. There were armed troops all around us. Oh, how I began to pray in the Spirit. Soon we were allowed to leave. No explanations were given, but the Lord spoke to me, "you shall see all sides of Me."

We met our contacts from Israel. We sang Jewish worship songs while they strummed their guitars. We had a long bus ride into Jerusalem. That night we gathered with about 200 other believers. After praise, the Lord gave me a vision in which he said to share with all present. The Lord showed me a silver domed building and that we were to anoint the scrolls and pillars. Then he said, "let His light (bright) shine in this dark place."

We stayed at the Americana Hotel right in the city near the gate to the Wailing Wall. It was old, but had class and tradition. Just outside of the hotel we found a flower garden. A man met us there from the hotel. I talked to him about Jesus and how excited I was to be here. Jerusalem is a very stony, dry, rocky place and gardens are a special blessing to have. Norman Vincent Peale had stayed at this hotel on all of his visits, the bell captain told us. I was assigned to room #8 with my friend. I new #8 in the Bible meant "new beginnings".

The next day, we went to the Wailing Wall. The women had to pray on one side and the men on the other. Three of us ladies were led to praise in tongues. Two of us were barefoot. My feet swelled so severely that I could not wear any shoes. I questioned the Holy Spirit. He said I was to be as a Joshua and possess the land. So I searched the Scriptures. While at the Wailing Wall, a Jewish woman said that we spoke Hebrew when we prayed. She told us to go to the High Synagogs for our calling was that of High Priestesses.

As we tried to leave the area, several people came up to us and said, "We must have the faith you have. What is it? How can we get it?" We told them it was Jesus. They must receive Jesus. They and others followed us and questioned us more. A Jewish couple came running up to us and asked, "What is your faith? We have been searching for this faith," they stated. The man grabbed my arm. He insisted, "Please tell me, I must know." Some countrymen began to yell at our tour guide. A Jewish Rabbi hurried over and was very upset. His loud screeches were translated to tell us that the couple had broken tradition. The Rabbi told them to leave us, but the couple remained with us. As we walked with them, we shared the love and truth of Jesus, the Living Word, The Messiah. The couple agreed in prayer and received Jesus. Our leader tried to calm down the Rabbi. Our leader told us to be very careful, so we were not thrown out of the area.

There was a glorious vision the Lord gave me at the Wailing Wall while other people were stuffing pieces of paper with prayer requests into the cracks in the wall. The Lord said, "Look, I am here with you". Then he showed me a huge opening he created in the wall. The Lord led men and women through the wall into a beautiful garden. The Lord told me to lead the people through the wall not just to it. He also said, "The walls are coming down so my people can go through and find my promises, and know my victory."

Next we came to a silver domed building. It was the exact place I had seen in the vision and given prophecy about. Before we entered, the Holy Spirit instructed us to anoint the scrolls. To our amazement, the place was being painted and the scrolls were all down on tables. So, we carefully took turns praying in the Spirit over all the scrolls. Just as we finished, a guard abruptly yelled, "What are you doing?" and told us not to touch anything.

After those two episodes, the three of us decided we did not want to cause any other disturbances, so we hesitated to enter the Dome of the Rock. One lady actually remained outside, but two of us got shoved in with the crowd. Our tour guide grabbed us and said not to be afraid and not to touch anything. I just knew the Lord wanted us in there and we were not to fear just obey the Lord. The Lord instructed me to tell my prayer partner to complete the circle in his name and possess the territory. The Lord said, "All tradition would be broken down in this dark place and He would be glorified."

Next I found two pieces of a broom thistle and a leaf by a pillar. So I made a cross with them and put the leaf on it. I then laid it on the red carpet that I was standing on. I was later told that the leaf was from a trumpet tree and this was symbolic of the threshing floor.

I was so deep into praise and worship of the Lord, Jesus when I heard the Holy Spirit say, "Will you be a spectacle for me?" I asked my prayer partner what this meant? She did not answer. In my heart I agreed to be whatever Jesus wanted me to be. Next my legs became weak, so I grabbed onto a pillar. My legs felt like solid rock. I could say nothing. I knew I was already slain in the Spirit. I recall lying there for a long time. The guards poured buckets of water over me. I kept praising the Lord in the Spirit, but no words would come out. I could hear a lot of noise and voices, but I could not move. Five guards tried to lift me up, but they could not move me. Someone said, "She's dead", another said, "She's a diabetic", another said, "She's in a coma". I was told that my face looked pale white.

Finally, our leader of the group broke through the crowd and laid hands on me and said, "She's slain in the Spirit. She's not sick or diabetic. It's Jesus here. It's God's presence." Next, the guards dumped another bucket of water on me.

More guards were summoned, armed with machine guns. About a half hour had passed. I was told that finally the guards were able to put me in a chair. I could not see anything but I could hear voices. They poured lots of water down my mouth, but I could not swallow. The Holy Spirit said, "You won't drown. I'm the Living Water. It's okay."

Some ladies said that I looked like a living cross, very white and dressed in bright red. Four guards carried me out in a chair. As I was carried out, I still could not see but I could speak. One of the ladies on the tour came over and laid hands on me. She was very upset. She said that I was a mess. I told her that I was fine. "It's Jesus, Jesus," I yelled loudly. I was told the guards seemed compassionate towards me and laid down their weapons. Fellow Christians fell into fear and confusion. I sat in my chair on the front entry of the Dome of the Rock. Many Jewish people asked what happened to me. I told them about Jesus, the Messiah. Yes,

I was sitting right there at the entry of the Dome of the Rock, surrounded by guards. The Arabs said it was a sign and said they wanted to know Jesus and they wanted to believe. A Jewish couple yelled out, "We have found the answer, Jesus."

Quickly, three members of our group dragged me to a nearby store. I could hardly stand up let alone walk. There the merchant said, "You are of the Lord. You have Jesus in you. I see Him in you." He took me to a place where there were beautiful gowns. The Lord said to hold up an elegant red velvet dress with pearls beaded on it. I then went to a mirror. The Lord said, "You are my princess." In the natural, I looked like a wet noodle but God saw me as a beautiful princess. I just had to worship the Lord. Word of the incident at the Dome spread all over the quarter. I was told that I had broken tradition in the Dome and was the first white woman ever slain there.

One of my lady friends who refused to go into the Dome with me decided to help me walk on. Our tour guide, Abraham, was filled with questions for me. Many others were questioning me. The tour guide was fearful of the guards and warned me not to cause any more incidents. Well, I was holding my lady friend's hand and suddenly she was slain in the Spirit. She fell right on the bare ground near St. Stephen's Gate. Children came running from all directions and circled us. The leader of our group came and laid hands on her and said she was slain in the Spirit. The Holy Spirit told me to lay hands on her forehead. Then I began speaking in another language. The Arab children began to answer me. One of them spoke English and interpreted. He said that I called them by their Arab names and spoke to them about Jesus and how much he loves them and that he died for them and now lives. Jesus wants to live in their hearts and forgives their sins. The children put out their hands and thirty of them began to say Jesus and point at their hearts. They nodded, Yes Jesus. So I prayed with each one as they put out their hands to receive Jesus. They became so happy. One boy doubted, but I spoke more Arabic to him. The others pushed him forward and he too nodded, yes Jesus. He became so peaceful and happy. These were truly miracles of salvation. Who would have thought that God would do miracles right in the Dome of the Rock and quarter!! The guards just walked by us the entire time and never even came over to see what was happening. Praise God.

My friend arose and began to dust herself off. She was very upset that everyone had just left us there all alone. Our leader came running to us to get us through the gate. It was locked as soon as we exited. My friend and the leader went ahead of me.

A countrywoman came up to me in the roadway. She had an eye missing and huge gray sores all over her arms and body. I was still so drugged in the Spirit that all I could say was "Jesus." As I touched the eye socket. She had received an eye. I touched her sores and said "Jesus" and the sores disappeared. Jesus performed a miracle on the spot. My leader, came hurriedly to me and said we had to leave quickly before the crowd could reach me. He said the lady was yelling "miracle". He said they would tear my clothing just to get a touch and a miracle now. All I felt was the presence of God and peace and joy. There were other miracles of salvation, healing, possessing the land, and breaking down strongholds. The Lord even gave me the big foot award. What a glorious day in the Lord and it was not over yet. In the next book, I will share many miracles and a great blessing that took place.

The Holy Spirit gave me prophecy while I was in Jerusalem, "You shall walk where no man shall go, for thy feet are strong and stand for Me. You honor Me and they shall receive. Heal my people, unite my people, teach my people. Arise my daughter, the trumpet sounds. Men shall respect and honor thee for great is thy status in Me."

Through all of the time in Israel, I learned that things are not as they appear, at first. I also learned to hear the voice of the Lord and obey Him!

A Matter of Life or Death

John 10:10 KJ "The thief comes that he might steal and may kill and destroy. I cam that they may have life and have it more abundantly to the full till it overflows."

Mark 16:18 KJ "They will lay hands on the sick and they will get well."

We had a prayer meeting at my home. As I prayed in my prayer language, the Holy Spirit spoke to me and said that it was urgent that I fly to Arizona to see Brother Weldon. He was the president of our church and ministers association. The Lord spoke that he was near death and to bind death and speak the life of Jesus into his weak body. The Lord also said He would supply all the needed funds. I only had child support at that time. During the prayer meeting, a lady said that God told her to give me the money I needed for this trip. This was a word of confirmation that it was urgent, a matter of life and death.

That very night I made arrangements to fly to Arizona. I called Brother Weldon's home and was informed that he was critically ill and in the hospital. When I arrived at the hospital there were several men outside the hospital room refusing to let me see Brother Weldon. I called out to Sister Weldon who was in the room and she insisted that they let me enter. I went to the bedside to pray with Brother Weldon, and one of the men tried to stop me. I put my hand out and said in the name of Jesus, the Lord sent me! The power of God hit the man and it looked as if someone swiftly pushed him on the next bed. He could not move. Then the men moved away from me.

As I prayed in the Spirit with Brother Weldon, he said he felt the presence of God and it was glorious. I spoke the Spirit of life in the name of Jesus and I told him that the Lord said he will live and be healed and must continue to do the work of God. Brother Weldon said, "Yes I will, Lord!" Tears flowed from his eyes and Sister Weldon began to cry and praise God. The Spirit of death was bound in the name of Jesus and Brother Weldon was whole and we knew it. The Holy Spirit told me to tell Sister Weldon to tell the doctor to do x-rays again and the blood test to prove the healing miracle. This was done the next day and all the tests were normal. Praise Jesus!

The man guarding the door kept bothering me. I discerned evil spirits. I warned Brother Weldon not to trust this man. Later it was proven that this man tried to take over the church association and even stole records and documents. Brother Weldon had to take legal action against him to save his ministry.

This day of the miracle healing was also the day of salvation and deliverance for the man that was pushed into the next bed by the power of God. When he came out of the room, he sat on the floor by the elevator and I sat down next to him. The Holy Spirit said to tell him he was no longer an alcoholic, he was free. JESUS SET HIM FREE. His wife came over to me and said that her husband had been a severe alcoholic for nineteen years. She was praising God for his salvation and deliverance. He became a wonderful husband and father. He was serving God and never took another drink. For over ten years, the family sent letters of victory and deliverance. The family had prayed for this man for twenty years and God heard their prayers, saved his soul, and set him free. NEVER GIVE UP! Keep praying for your loved ones. God won't fail you. The prayer of the righteous man availeth much! The devil can't keep our families in bondage any longer. Jesus gave us the victory.

Brother Weldon left the hospital in three days. He was healed and whole. For many years he continued to lead over seven hundred churches and ministers in serving the Lord and spreading the gospel of Jesus Christ. He also was a loving mentor to me. He is now in heaven with Jesus.

David's Healings

Mark 16:18 KJ "They shall take up serpents and if they drink any deadly thing it shall not hurt them, they shall lay hands on the sick and they shall recover.

When David was just 13 years old, he went to Guadalajara, Mexico with a neighbor from Mexico. While in Mexico, David became violently ill with a 105-degree fever. I was called several times to come and get him and fly him to the states. He was getting worse. At that time, I did not have any money. So, I prayed with my neighbor on the telephone for Jesus to heal David. He is a believer, and laid hands on David as we prayed. Jesus answered our prayers even though we were a thousand of miles apart.

David returned home somewhat weak and tired, but gave us a wonderful report. He had completed his assignment and delivered Spanish Bibles to Mexico that we obtained in Jerusalem, the Holy Land. The Mexican people were so very blessed with the Bibles. David was our first missionary from our church.

God Spares David's Life

We had just attended church. It was a wonderful time of praise and worship. About 1500 people were there. Next, we prepared to go on a trip up into Canada by boat.

We were blessed with a 36-foot salon cabin cruiser. Our children had been brought up on boat safety. Toward, evening, I was putting away food and supplies for the trip. I was inside the front of the boat. I heard a splash and knew to run to the back. When I arrived, my husband had just felt led of God to reach down next to the dock. He grabbed what he felt. It turned out to be David's hair. It was dark. If God had not intervened, we were told we would not have found him for days. Again, the Lord's hand was on David. He spared his life. Well the next morning, we still decided to go on the trip. The mechanics had worked on the gas tanks and filled them to capacity. There was a sniffer on the boat that did not ever work, but my husband decided to try it anyhow. It showed gas fumes at a high volume. My husband ran through the boat and opened up the area of the gas tanks. The bilge was filled with gas. If Dave had started the engines the entire marina would have exploded especially, since we were next to the gas station. I don't know how many lives were saved that day, but I truly believed God was with and watching over us. The sniffer never ever gave a reading again, just that one time.

David's Back Is Healed

David was about 9 years old and was invited to his friend's house for a birthday party. The boys decided to play hide and seek. David loved to climb trees, and this time he found a great tree to hide in. While he was up in the tree he heard a cracking sound. Before he could grab a hold, the branch broke, tossing him about 10 feet to the ground. I was called and rushed over. David could not move and was crying loudly. Other children were screaming. I had the mother call the doctor. I then laid hands on David for a miracle healing. David even prayed with me. I asked all of the children to call on Jesus to heal him, and they did.

Next, since there was not an ambulance service in town, I had to take him to the hospital. I got an ironing board and we lifted David into the back of my station wagon. The doctor said if he had landed anywhere else, his back would have been fractured. David said it felt like the angel just put him down on the ground between the metal swing set and other things. He just missed the swing set by a couple of inches.

When we arrived at the hospital, David could not stand up and had a paralysis. We called the elders of the church for prayer. Within 24 hours, he was feeling great, no fractures, the pain left. He was just thanking the Lord and praising Him, and so was I!

Miracle of Music For Susan

I Samuel 23:16 KJ "Prince Jonathan now went to find David; He met him at Horesh and encouraged him to his faith in God.

Galatians 6:2 LB "Share each other's troubles and problems, and so obey our Lord's command.

Psalm 150:3,6 KJ "Praise him with the trumpet (horn) and the lute and the harp. Let everything alive give praises to the Lord.

My daughter, Susan should be called the "daughter of encouragement" just as Barnabus was called the "son of encouragement" by the apostles. He gave unselfishly of himself to others. This was like my beautiful daughter. Susan was "Miss Inspiration" to everyone. When she was about six years old, a prophecy had come forth about her gift of music and she learned to play both the piano and the organ, but never had piano lessons.

When Susan was in sixth grade, she chose to play the French horn. Susan was a petite girl and could hardly lift the French horn. I remember her practicing diligently and turning blue from lack of air as she practiced. The French horn has over eighteen feet of tubing. She often wanted to quit, but she never gave up. She prayed to the Lord for strength.

There also was a prophecy that we would be called the "Trumpet of Triumph" family. The following year, my son David starting playing the trombone in band and showed remarkable talent. My niece who lived with us chose to play trumpet. She also excelled in music throughout high school. Her twin brothers played trumpet also. Yes we are the "Trumpets of Triumph" just as God's word of prophecy had called us. Tom, my youngest son, also played trumpet.

Our church was small and everyone participated. David would lead worship and five year-old Tom was the usher, Susan was our organist. She only had one year of lessons, but she practiced constantly. Susan was greatly blessed in music. She would play victory and worship songs on the organ when things became too difficult for us. Susan's music always encouraged us. We had church in our home twice a week, and we had seven children and my sister living with us. We fought the fight of faith continuously to keep the church and the ministry.

Susan wanted to do a Christian musical called "The Witness". She made sure we all had parts and practiced every day. Our favorite song was "The Victor". Once in the middle of a storm in downtown Capac, Susan played "The Victor", and the Lord sent sunshine. We had a local town celebration. Susan helped me get a Christian band together to share the Gospel right on the street and she arranged for Christian musicians to come into her high school to share the word of God. In this conservative rural community, this was indeed a miracle.

Susan dedicated all her music to glorify the Lord. She even stated in our Church newsletter, "My purpose in playing music is to serve and praise the Lord… His love makes music alive and special." Soon she had my son and niece performing little songs on their instruments to praise the Lord. She always encouraged us to praise and trust God. I thank the Holy Spirit for the gift of wisdom that my daughter so often shared. It was a blessing.

We lived in a farming community. There were no opportunities for music and it was next to impossible to find music teachers. However, it was prophesied that Susan would perform in huge auditoriums and in Orchestra Hall, which was not even renovated then.

When Susan went to college she was required to take piano. She never studied piano, but was self-taught on the organ with the

Lord's help. We prayed for a miracle and we got it. Susan aced a 4.0 grade point average in college piano, and was highly honored by her college professor. Where did this gift come from? The professor said it was impossible to achieve this ability on the piano without years of training. We know that God gave the miracle that Susan needed. The Lord is faithful and true to His promise!

Susan became a gifted French hornist. She won scholarships and funds made it possible for her to study with the principal French hornist of the Detroit Symphony Orchestra. She entered many competitions and received state awards. She received first prize at a Canadian Music Festival. She performed at the All State Band camp, the World Youth Symphony and the State Fair Honors Band. She was a member of The International Symphony Orchestra of Port Huron and Canada, the University of Michigan Youth Orchestra and other orchestras. Susan auditioned and was chosen to perform in the Detroit Symphony Civic Orchestra for three years.

During this time, I was going through a divorce and my sister Bethy was murdered. She was only seventeen. Earlier I had been my sister's guardian and Susan and Bethy had shared a room together.

Susan was my oldest of the seven children in my home. She could organize any situation. She helped with all the chores. She had much responsibility and still managed to graduate fourth in her class. I thanked the Lord for her constantly. She truly was a gift from the Lord. Her encouragement and inspiration kept me going.

Susan became a gifted music and vocal teacher. She earned a masters degree in education and she continues to perform in many symphony orchestras. Music professionals request her and applaud her musical gift and talent. Susan's favorite scripture is Psalm 150.

The Miracle of Salvation

John 3:16-17 KJ "For God so loved the world that He gave His only begotten Son, that whoever believes in Him should not perish but have everlasting life. For God did not send His Son into the world to condemn the world, but that the world through Him might be saved."

The person closest to my heart that I was able to lead to the Lord Jesus was my seventeen year-old Sister, Bethy. She grew up without a father and our mother worked all the time to pay the rent and support five children. Bethy was the youngest of the five children and was very independent. She had a hard time adjusting to school. Bethy was a bright young lady and expressed her self in art. The other children were in high school when she was born. By the time Bethy was thirteen she had been raped. A twenty-eight year old man who was supposedly a friend of our family, introduced her to drugs. Bethy went out on the streets and never finished high school. It broke my heart to see her this way. I was given guardianship of Bethy and she began attending school and making friends, but our mother took me to court and caused problems with everyone we knew causing great turmoil. The judge said it was better to give her back to my mother and save my family all this distress. The judge also said Bethy probably would die before she reached the age of eighteen. Since their home was a total wreck in a bad neighborhood, we told my mother we would help them move to an area with better living conditions. My mother refused our help. She even kept me from seeing Bethy for three years even though I had a court order to see her regularly.

When Bethy was seventeen, she became pregnant. She got off drugs, and was so excited about the baby. When she called me, I offered to have her live with us and to give her any help that she might need. Just before she was due to have her baby, she was set up by past friends and was arrested. I was able to talk to her for two hours on the phone that weekend.

Bethy's baby was born two weeks early. One day the Lord spoke to me. He told me to drop everything that I was doing and to go see Bethy. So I cleaned up the children, bought Bethy flowers and gifts for Bethy and the baby, and drove to Detroit to visit her. She was asleep when I arrived. I did not understand the urgency of the Holy Spirit to visit Bethy that day. I talked with her and then felt led to pray with her. She recommitted her life to Jesus as her Savior and asked for forgiveness. She had accepted the Lord when she was a child living with me, but back slid over the years. She cried as she prayed the sinner's prayer. I asked her to come and stay with us, but she refused. We had a wonderful time seeing Bethy and her baby, and I knew in my heart that she was forgiven and saved. I never saw Bethy alive again. Two days later, she was murdered in Detroit near her home. We had to hide Bethy's baby because we learned of a baby black market that wanted to sell her baby.

I felt anger, grief, and sorrow, but I knew I could feel joy because Bethy was with Jesus. The devil had tried all of her life to destroy her, but Jesus reached out and saved her. I am thankful that my children saw her praying and rejoicing. They will remember her as being happy and loving her baby.

The Lord gave me a vision of Bethy: I saw her dancing before the Lord. Her long brown hair moved with the wind and she was robed in a beautiful white garment. She had a smile on her face, and I knew that she truly was with Jesus and was totally rejoicing.

We just never know how long we have to live. That is why we must know that we are saved, our sins forgiven, and that we will have eternal life with Jesus Christ. We may have an hour, a minute, a day or years, but receiving the salvation of Jesus Christ cannot wait. Bethy only had me to pray with her and only two more days to live. Praise God, she made the right decision and now she will spend eternity with God in heaven. She did not risk her future. She knew Jesus is real and loved her and died for her sins. She wanted eternal life with him. Bethy is finally happy and safe eternally.

From Surgeries To Scholar

Isaiah 54:4-6 KJ "Fear not for you will no longer live in shame. The shame of your youth and the sorrows of your widowhood will be remembered no more. For your creator will be your husband." The Lord of Hosts is His name, He is the Redeemer, the Holy One of Israel, the God of all the Earth. For the Lord has called you back from your grief— a young wife abandoned by her husband.

Psalm 119:25 IB "I am completely discouraged—I lie in the dust. Revive me by Your Word. I told you my plans and you replied. Now give me your instructions. Make me understand what you want; for then I shall see your miracles."

I Peter 5:6,7 KJ "Humble yourselves therefore under the mighty hand of God that He may exalt you in due time. Casting all your care upon Him; for He cares for you.

After my husband, who was manic-depressive, divorced me again, the Christian therapist advised me to take some college courses. She set up a special funding through the state office for me to complete an Associates degree plus a Bachelor of Science with a major and minor. It was a day-to-day challenge. I still spent most of my time in the wheelchair and was on many medications, plus physical therapy. The agency arranged for me to get hand controls to drive, and training to use them. The community college was a 38 mile drive each way and the university was 48 miles each way. Some mornings I could not wake up and had to stop for coffee several times just to get to a class. I was blessed with tutors. My memory was so dulled from medications. I fought arthritic pain continuously in my back, wrists, shoulders, and neck that never stopped complaining. There were not many provisions made for handicap persons at either college. I remember the exhaustion I felt by the time I got my wheel chair from the parking lot to the door. Most days I just wanted to turn around and go home and forget this craziness. I knew I had been out of the job market for a few years and needed skills. How would I take care of Thomas, who was about eight or nine years old? I did not have any relatives that cared about us. After the surgeries, very few friends came around or called to visit. It was a desperately lonely, frightening situation. Here I was a Christian minister, who spent years doing outreach ministries for others, and now where did everyone go? I called other churches about widow or single mom programs, but did not find any to help. The only thing I was offered by the government was more education no matter what physical condition I was in. The program was set up as if I had no disabilities, I should be in college classes preparing for some great job in the future. So I thanked the Lord for the open door and decided to give it my very best effort.

Every evening I would pack my ankle and neck in ice bags to slow down the pain and then I would begin my homework.

My concentration skills were so limited that I would set a timer for 20 minutes, take a 5 minute- break and start over again. My eyes would blur from medications and I had to change positions frequently to stop aches and pains, cramps in my legs and other areas. I would start off with much prayer and ask the Holy Spirit to help me and bring to remembrance what I needed. I wrote my notes from the tape recording of classes and I rewrote them many times to understand the material. I knew I could not fail and must keep seeking God to help me. I could not do any housework the days that I had classes, or I'd be too exhausted to drive. It felt like discipline upon discipline. I kept pushing a body and mind that strongly resisted and resented my drive.

For typing, I requested special equipment but it did not arrive until the final exam. Somehow the Lord got me through it. I had a neck brace, a back brace, an ankle brace, and a hand brace. Can you believe I even dared to go to typing class? I surely was a spectacle so I usually tried to sit in back. I usually required pain medication after class. In spite of my get up, would you believe I won a speed typing award one day in class.

Well I was blessed to get my Associate degree. The head of admissions met with me and saw my transcript from Wayne State University that showed three years of classes. He arranged for me to take the 5 courses and receive my degree with highest honors. This was a time of triumph for me. I had also been a member of the honor society. I began to feel a sense of worth again. The Lord had made it possible for me to graduate with honors.

Well the divorce continued in the court, so I started classes at U of M Flint. I was doing fairly well. The classes were at night and 3 hours long each. I quickly discovered I had been sheltered from the world's condition around me as I studied political health issues and environmental health. It was the week before finals and my daughter got hit at Michigan State Campus. The next week, a man tried to physically attack her in a parking lot in broad day light on campus. She hit him with her French horn in the name of Jesus and he took flight. God had truly protected her from serious injury in both situations. I could only thank the Lord for saving my daughter. It was emotionally hard on her, but she is such a trooper and finished her studies with all "A's". I just had to be with her to help her cope, so I applied for incompletes. I was turned down in one main course, and so I started out with an "E" in one of my courses. I was somewhat devastated. The divorce was requiring so much time. Lawyers were driving us crazy with testimonies, bills, and office meetings.

I asked the Lord what to do, and He gave me favor to take the course over again. I was thus blessed with an "A". The miracle in all of this was that the scholarship monies were not taken away from me even with a failing grade. I spent much of my time, especially while driving, in prayer. I always had praise and worship music tapes on as I drove. I knew with God's help, I would make it safely to campus. The next challenge was to make it from the car to the classroom. There were no conveniences for handicappers, no special doors, ramps, bathrooms, or computers. Praise God there was an elevator, but I had to educate the students to let me use it. They would all push on and leave me sitting there. I had to change this or I'd never get to a class. I was totally disappointed by the unreceptive, unhelpful staff. After 3 years, the disabilities agency did put pressure on the university to make changes. God taught me to recruit helpers on campus with my wheelchair and I met many special people this way. I always had my "I love Jesus" stickers on my chair in plain sight. Many students told me this was great. I wanted to witness for the Lord and this was a small way.

Soon, I was having prayer support meetings with several of the ladies right there on campus. So many ladies had lost jobs and were in there 40's and 50's returning to college. Most had children to care for and had divorces. So many were on Prozac and other medications desperately trying to make it through so they could get jobs. Many tears flowed at the prayer meetings. Some had lost everything. Some ladies had been in professions for years and found their positions eliminated. At times, I felt as if God had me there for these ladies. They needed to know Jesus did not abandon them as friends and relatives did. They needed to hear the Word of God and know He cared. Some needed God's salvation. God gave me grace to encourage them and show His love to them. What a mission field! I helped set up a women's center on campus and was on the board of a city shelter for abuse, chairperson of the university of women, on selection committees for staff. I witnessed strongly to a professor, who was a top administrator and shared the compassion of Jesus toward women. She and I prayed often together after that and learned to listen to Christian music on our long drives. She became a wonderful Christian friend.

Right in the middle of a big city, at a big university, a handicapped lady in a wheelchair was given the privilege to share the love of Jesus and help these ladies. I began to look forward to class days more and more. I was excited to see what the Lord had waiting for me and He always had someone who needed His love. I graduated with honors and Scholar awards from University of Michigan.

Conclusion

Revelations 12:11 KJ "And they overcame him by the blood of the Lamb, and by the word of their testimony; and they loved not their lives unto the death.

Jesus cares for you. I have shared some of the wonderful miracles the Lord had given to me. There were so many others He did for me including saving my life from car accidents, protecting me from spies, con artists, dangers that I never expected. He provided miracle monies and food supplies so many times for me. Well, I'll just have to write another book to share the other exciting miracles in my life. I pray this book has encouraged your faith, given you hope, and made you want to praise God with me.

Now it is your turn to receive miracles that you need in your life. The greatest miracle is salvation. Are you forgiven of your sins? Is Jesus in your heart? Is Jesus your Savior? If not, today is the day to accept Jesus, repent and be saved. God loves you so much. You are so valuable and special to Him. Open your heart and accept Him now. Next, make Jesus Lord of your life. Study the Word. Pray to the Lord. Fellowship with Him, because it is God's will to bless us.

Nothing is impossible with God and all things are possible to you if you believe God and His Word. No miracle is to little or too big for God to do. BEGIN YOUR MIRACLE WALK WITH GOD TODAY!! MAKE A LIST OF THE MIRACLES YOU NEED. I WILL BE HAPPY TO PRAY WITH YOU FOR THE MIRACLES YOU NEED. John 3:16

THE MIRACLE OF SALVATION

John 3:16 For God so loved the world that He gave His only begotten Son, that whoever believes in Him should not perish but have everlasting life. (NKJ)

Romans 10:9 that if you confess with your mouth the Lord Jesus and believe in your heart that God has raised Him from the dead, you will be saved. (NKJ)

God loves you very much and He wants you to go to Heaven. That is why He sent Jesus.

Jesus, the Son of God, died on the cross to forgive your sins and give you eternal life.

Now pray this prayer with me to receive the greatest miracle.

Heavenly Father please forgive me of my sins. I believe that Jesus is the Son of God and died on the cross for me. I also believe that He rose from the dead and is alive today. I ask you, Jesus to come into my heart as my Savior and Lord. I thank you for the gift of eternal life and my sins are forgiven. I am saved. Please empower me with your Holy Spirit that I may live and serve you as Lord of my life.

Now write to me and tell me that you have accepted Jesus as your Lord and Savior. Read John chapter 3 verse 16 and Romans chapter 10, verse 9.

Send me any prayer requests so that we can believe together for God's miracles in your life.

WRITE TO:

CAPAC CHRISTIAN FELLOWSHIP
Rev. Helen Petipren
32505 Parker Circle
Warren, Michigan 48088.